Dedication

This book is dedicated to all children and adults in the diaspora who are searching for the truth about their history and identity. This book is also dedicated to the Lion of the Tribe of Judah; without your sacrifice, none of this would be possible.

"For I knew that they would not hear Me, because it is a stiff-necked people; but in the land of their captivities they shall remember themselves." Book of Baruch 2:30

“Good morning, everyone, I am your guest teacher, Ms. Marcellus; I will be teaching you History this period. Your regular teacher will not be here for a few weeks, but I am looking forward to a lot of new learning experiences with you during her absence.”

“History can be a dry and boring subject for some students; however, I believe that it is an exciting subject, and I look forward to making it exciting for you. We will be veering from the regular outline and discussing the history of different cultures including your own. I will be assigning you a couple of projects that you will work on in teams of two regarding your cultural or ethnic backgrounds.”

Candace raised her hand and asked, “Ms. Marcellus, can we choose our teammates for the projects, or are you going to assign us partners?”

“You can choose your own partners, but if anyone does not have a partner, I will assign them a partner. For the first project, you will interview your teammate to find out about their culture and ethnicity. I want you to do some research after they tell you about their ethnic backgrounds and you will share a historical fact about what you learned about that ethnicity or culture with the class,” advised Ms. Marcellus.

“Okay everyone, I want you to choose a partner to work with on the project; once you have chosen someone, raise your hand if you don’t have a partner. I will give you a few minutes to choose someone,” said Ms. Marcellus.

“I don’t see any hands raised to indicate that you don’t have a partner. That must mean that everyone has a partner?”, asked Ms. Marcellus

The students said yes in unison.

“That’s great; I will call each student up to my desk so I can write down who is working together on the project,” said Ms. Marcellus.

Candace approached Ms. Marcellus first to let her know that she was paired with Steven.

“Hi Ms. Marcellus, I am Candace. Steven and I will be working together. “

“Hello Candace. Does that mean that you are going to take the lead in this project?” asked Ms. Marcellus. “No, we will work on it as a team.” “That’s what I like to hear Candace, teamwork is best on a project like this,” said Ms. Marcellas.

“Can you tell me a little about your ethnic background so that I can do my own research to add to what you share with the class?” asked Ms. Marcellus. Candace exclaimed, I am a Hebrew

Israelite and we will talk about our culture as Hebrews from the lineage of Shem and of the tribe of Judah!" "We are not Hebrews as far as religion, but our ethnicity is Hebrew", added Candace.

"I am really looking forward to what you will share with the class regarding your ethnic background as Hebrew Israelites, children. I will do my own research to add to the end of your presentation," stated Ms. Marcellus.

"There is so much we can share with the class" exclaimed Steven. "Yes, but according to the instructions for the project, we only have 10 minutes to give the presentation," said Candace. "Yeah, that is not a lot of time," said Steven. "We both have to share so we can use 20 minutes, 10 minutes each," said Candace. "Well, we don't have to go all the way back to when our forefathers lived in Israel; we can start with their escape from Jerusalem." Candace said. "Okay, let's start there since that explains how we arrived in West Afrika and then they were captured years later and brought on ships to America and other countries in the world," added Steven. "Alright, let's do it!" exclaimed Candace.

Candace told Steven that they should include visuals in the presentation. "We should have a map of Israel that shows their exodus when our forefathers fled from the Babylonians and they escaped into West Afrika." "Yes, we should do that and instead of calling it Afrika, why not call it by the original name of the continent which was Alkebulan," stated Steven. "You know it was the original place of the garden of Eden written about in the bible," he added. "Oh yes, that's a good point," said Candace, and we should explain that Alkebulan means "the garden of Eden" and it also means "mother of mankind."

"Let's show the original map that demonstrates that our forefathers built a kingdom there in West Alkebulan known as the Kingdom of Judah, located North of the Gold Coast also known today as Ghana", added Steven. "Okay, that sounds like a good idea", stated Candace, but then we will have to talk about the 12 tribes of Israel so that the class understands that there was a separation among the tribes of Israel and some of the descendants remained with Israel and others remained with Judah", Steven said. "I'll work on a chart that shows the 12 tribes of Israel; do you want to work on the map showing the exodus?" asked Candace. "Yes, I will work on that", said Steven

ALKEBULAN

The Garden of Eden; Mother of Mankind

The day of the presentation came; Steven and Candace were ready, and they presented their project. Candace started by telling the class that she and Steven, did their project on their ethnicity as Hebrew Israelites from the tribe of Judah. The whole class was silent and attentive. Steven said, "I know some of you may have questions about what we are about to share, and we will be glad to answer your questions at the end if Ms. Marcellus allows us."

"Yes, if there are any questions, the class has 10 minutes to ask them after your presentation. I will also be adding some information once the questions have concluded", Ms. Marcellus stated.

Hebrew Israelites From The Tribe Of Judah

Jacob who was renamed Israel/Yasharal had two wives, Leah and Rachel. From his marriage with Leah, Israel had 8 sons:

Reuben, Simeon. Levi, Judah, Gad, Asher, Issachar, and Zebulan.

Gad and Asher were born from Leah's maidservant, Zilpah with Israel; Leah and Israel only had 6 sons together)

From Israel's marriage to Rachel were born 4 sons:

Dan, Naphtali, Joseph, and Benjamin

Dan and Naphtali were born from Rachel's maidservant Bilhah with Israel; Rachel and Israel only had 2 sons together, Joseph and Benjamin.

Candace explained, "Our forefathers had to flee from Israel because after the Babylonians destroyed the temple there, they began to massacre our people. They fled through Afrika which was known as Alkebulan; it means the garden of Eden or the mother of mankind. Many names on the continent of Alkebulan were changed so going forward we will refer to Afrika by its original name, Alkebulan."

Steven further added, "Our people scattered throughout Alkebulan, but the tribe of Judah settled northeast of the Gold Coast which is known today as Ghana." "It was here that they established a new kingdom, known as the Kingdom of Judah or Ouidah since there is no "J" in our Hebrew language. We settled there, but because of our traditions of worship and culture were different from the Alkebulans that lived there, we were viewed as outsiders. Today that land is called Togo and Benin." Candace interjected by saying, "The "slave coast" is written under the Kingdom of Judah which tells us that most of the people taken in the transatlantic slave trade came from there. It was also prophesied that our forefathers would be taken into slavery again because of their failure to observe the covenant that God made with them. We don't have time to read Deuteronomy in the Torah to show you all the curses that came upon our forefathers, but it is written that the curses would be a sign and wonder for all the nations to know that we are the Hebrew Israelites from the tribe of Judah."

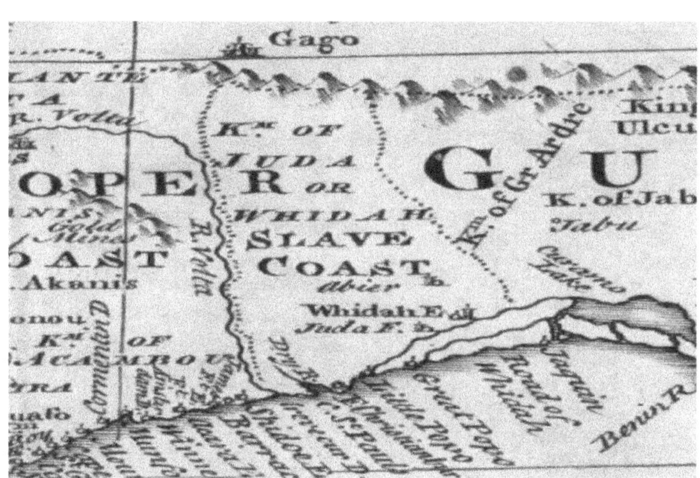

"As you can see from this ancient map, this was also where the transatlantic slave trade occurred. Many of the people captured for this slave trade were from the tribe of Judah. The Alkebulans, were approached by Portuguese, British, and French men who were looking to buy slaves. Since our forefathers were considered outsiders, some of the Alkebulan kings made pacts with the European slave traders that they would give them our people in exchange for tobacco, guns and ammunition, and alcohol. Hebrew men and women were captured and handed over to the slave traders, stated Candace.

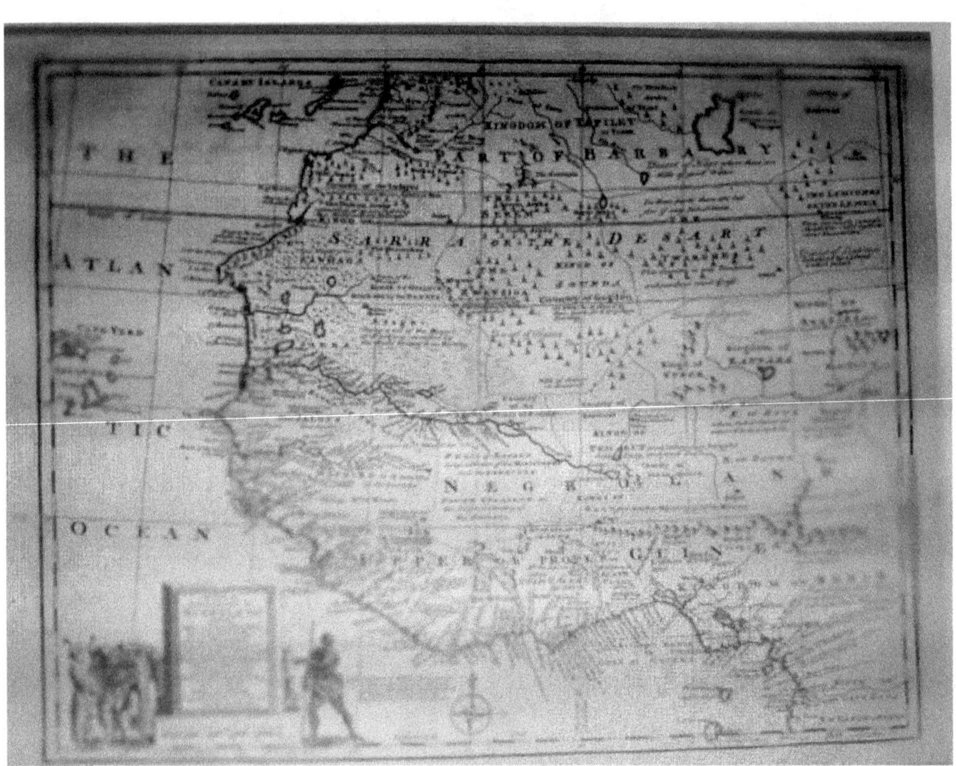

Candace stated, “on this ancient map you will see “Negroland”, the Zondervan Bible

Dictionary tells us that Ham was the progenitor of the dark races such as the Egyptians, Ethiopians, Libyans, and Canaanites but not the Negro. The negro is believed to be the Shemites since we know that Noah had 3 sons, they were Ham, Shem, and Japheth. All

the people groups in the world are descended from one of the 3 sons. They were all considered Black but it is also believed that Japheth was an albino since the Book of Enoch says that Noah didn’t look like his brethren and from the description it provides of him, having white skin and white hair and it was like wool, he was an albino.”

“Yes, said Steven, Ham was the father or progenitor of the dark races that Candance named, Shem was the progenitor of the Hebrew Israelites, and Japheth was the progenitor of the Europeans. Since those with albinism have a problem with being in the sun, it is believed that Japheth migrated North to the European areas because it was a colder climate, and the sun was not as harsh as it was in the areas surrounding Alkebulan where Ham and Shem’s descendants lived.”

“That concludes our presentation”, stated Steven. Candace said, “We will be glad to answer questions now.”

Steven called on Mikael since they were best friends, and he was the only boy with a raised hand. "Mikael, I see your hand raised, what do you want to ask?" "I really enjoyed your presentation, but how can you be Hebrew Israelites when the people in Israel are not Black?", asked Mikael. "That's a good question", said Steven. "The people who are living in Israel who are Caucasians are from the lineage of Japheth; they are known as Ashkenazi Jews who are converts of the Hebrew or Jewish religion. They are not ethnically Hebrew Israelites from the 12 tribes of our forefathers or the progenitor of our ancestors", said Steven.

Candace added, "Yes, they are Khazars from Khazaria; they converted to Judaism because they didn't find Islam or Christianity appealing. Remember, we are Hebrew Israelites, ethnically, not religiously. We follow the Christian faith, but our ethnicity is Hebrew."

Candace called on another student, Shayla, who had her hand raised. Before Shayla could ask her question, Ms. Marcellus cautioned the class that time was short so Shayla's question would be the last one but any students who wanted further clarification, could speak with Steve and Candace during recess.

Shayla stated that she only had a short question to ask. "You said that there were curses placed on the Hebrew Israelites, can you tell us one that would convince us that what you are saying is a sign and wonder as you mentioned?" Again, Ms. Marcellus interjected by saying, "I will be going over some of the curses that will let you know that what Candace and Steven presented is accurate and historical information. Okay, class, that was the last question for our presenters, let's give them applause for the great job that they did.

The classroom erupted into applause and Stephen and Candace gathered up their resource materials and headed back to their seats. Next, Ms. Marcellus went to the blackboard and began writing on it. After completing the writing, she turned to the class.

Ms. Marcellus said, "Not everyone accepts the truths in the bible or in the Torah. What we will look at next to bring clarity about what was presented are the curses in Deuteronomy; they will demonstrate to you that what occurred with the transatlantic slave trade was prophesied or foretold. If you want to do your own research, I have written on the blackboard all the scriptures that I will be sharing. Do your own research; I am sure you will see that it all lines up with history.

Deuteronomy 28:15 But it shall come to pass, if you do not obey the voice of the LORD your God, to observe carefully all His commandments and His statutes which I command you today, that all these curses will come upon you and overtake you.

Deuteronomy 28:45-46 Moreover all these curses shall come upon thee, and shall pursue thee, and overtake thee, till thou be destroyed; because thou hearkened not unto the voice of the LORD thy God, to keep his commandments and his statutes which he commanded thee:

46 And they shall be upon thee for a sign and for a wonder, and upon thy seed forever.

Deuteronomy 28; 48 Therefore shalt thou serve thine enemies which the LORD shall send against thee, in hunger, and in thirst, and in nakedness, and in want of all *things*: and he shall put a yoke of iron upon thy neck until he has destroyed thee."

Deuteronomy 28;64 And the LORD shall scatter thee among all people, from the one end of the earth even unto the other; and there thou shalt serve other gods, which neither thou nor thy fathers have known, *even* wood and stone.

Deuteronomy 28;30 Thou shalt betroth a wife, and another man shall lie with her: thou shalt build a house, and thou shalt not dwell therein: thou shalt plant a vineyard, and shalt not gather the grapes thereof.

Deuteronomy 28; 32 Thy sons and thy daughters *shall be* given unto another people, and thine eyes shall look, and fail *with longing* for them all the day long: and *there shall be* no might in thine hand.

Deuteronomy 28:41 Thou shalt beget sons and daughters, but thou shalt not enjoy them; for they shall go into captivity.

"These are some of the curses mentioned in the bible regarding the Hebrew Israelites. We know that during the transatlantic slave trade, all these things happened to what the world calls Afrikan Americans and other slaves that were taken to other countries throughout the world," added Ms. Marcellus.

"Remember that the scripture said that the curses would be a **SIGN and a WONDER** regarding the Israelites. None of these curses came upon the people that refer to themselves as Jews. They had a Holocaust, but it was not like these curses that came upon my forefathers," added Candace.

Deuteronomy 28:49-50 The LORD shall bring a nation against thee from far, from the end of the earth, *as swift* as the eagle fly's a nation whose tongue thou shalt not understand; A nation of fierce countenance, which shall not regard the person of the old, nor show favor to the young.

Deuteronomy 28:68 And the LORD shall bring thee into Egypt again with ships, by the way whereof I spoke unto thee, Thou shalt see it no more again: and there ye shall be sold unto your enemies for bondmen and bondwomen, and no man shall buy *you.*

Ms. Marcellus paused to explain this scripture. "Egypt means bondage; so, in this curse, the Israelites were to go into bondage again but this time it would be by ships, and they would see their land no more. When it says "no man shall buy you"; it means that no man would redeem them from slavery or purchase their freedom.

Leviticus 26:38 And you shall perish among the heathen, and the land of your enemies shall eat you up.

Ms. Marcellus ended speaking; she looked out at the class of students who were looking at her in amazement. One student raised her hand,

“Ms. Marcellus, the things that you just spoke about really does sound like what happened to the slaves that were brought over in the transatlantic slave trade”, Patti said.

“Yes, that is why the scriptures say that these curses would be a sign and a wonder regarding who the Hebrew Israelites are”, stated Ms. Marcellus. She further added, “there are many indications that what Steven and Candace shared about their ethnic identity and that of their forefathers being Hebrew Israelites is true.

“One of the standing churches that the slaves built in Savannah, Georgia was the First African Baptist Church has Hebrew writing on the sides of the pews that was written by the slaves. It was said that the slaves were illiterate, but they weren’t. They had a language which was Hebrew; they did not understand English and when they used their language or practiced any of their cultural beliefs, the slave owners punished them so that they would adopt the traditions and language of the slave owners and forget their own. You must also understand that the Hebrew language was not revived in America until the year 1881 and the church with the Hebrew writing by the Hebrew slaves was built in 1788,” explained Ms. Marcellus.

Steven exclaimed, "the nation that has come against my people, the Hebrew Israelites spoken of in Deuteronomy 28:49-50, when it says that they are "from the end of the earth as swift as the eagle fly's, a nation whose tongue (which means language) you shall not understand", sounds like the U.S. since their national symbol is the eagle, doesn't it? The forefathers didn't understand English, they spoke the Hebrew language. The church that you mentioned, Ms. Marcellus with the Hebrew writing on the pews verifies that they knew and spoke Hebrew and were not illiterate."

Ms. Marcellus looked at Steven and nodded, yes.

Another student raised his hand and asked, "If what you are saying is true, how is it that the people in Israel are Caucasian?" asked Scott.

"The people who live in Israel are not Israelites from the 12 tribes of YasharAl (Israel). YasharAl was known as Jacob before God changed his name to YasharAl/Israel; those people are Israelis not Israelites. Many of them follow the religion of Judaism and they are converts to the religion, not ethnically Israelites"; I will provide more details about them in our next class, said Ms. Marcellus.

The bell rang notifying the students that it was time for recess. Ms. Marcellus advised the students that if they had any other questions, they could ask her after recess or speak with Steven and Candace who might be able to answer their questions.

"Hey, wasn't that a really good presentation by Candace and Steven?," asked Joseph. "Yes, it was," replied David. "But I have one question that keeps bothering me", said Joseph. "Why doesn't anyone talk about this, and the people who converted to Judaism who are in Israel, why are they viewed as the true Jews", asked Joseph.

"It's kind of a long story", replied David; it all started in the 8th century. The Khazars who lived in Europe around Germany were a pagan group of people. During that time, the Roman empire was strong, and Islam was as well along with Judaism. On one side of the land of Khazaria, the Romans were insisting that people convert to their religion, on the other side, Islam was trying to convert people as well. The Israelites were also gaining converts to Judaism. After the prince of the Khazars reviewed all the teachings and practices of the different religions, he chose Judaism and he demanded that all his subjects convert as well. But instead of leaving it as it was, over time, the Khazars mixed the Hebrew religion with other beliefs from the Talmud and came up with a form of Judaism", explained David. "The term "Jewish" does not exist in the Hebrew language because there is no "J", so it was a term that was made up to explain that it was not a pure Hebrew belief system".

"Yes, I know it's amazing information that people don't discuss. They take it at face value that because so many people converted, that they are the original people of the religion, but they are not and what they practice is not what our forefathers practiced. They became known as Ashkenazi Jews from Khazaria and they settled in the area that is being called Israel. You must remember, Israel only became a state in 1948; that is not that long ago."

"I could tell you so much more about the history of our people, but recess is nearly over, and we need to get back inside. I will give you some book titles that you can get in the library that will explain more about everything," added David. "Cool, that would be great," said Joseph. "One of the books that I have in mind is entitled, "The Jews: A Study of Race and Environment", by Maurice Fishberg written in 1911. In this book it discusses the problem that anthropologists had with the concept of Indo-Germanic people finding their way into the midst of a dark-complexioned race like the Jews", explained David.

"The problem with that is that we are not Jews; we are Judaeans from the tribe of Judah. The term "Jews" was only recently created just as "Israel" was only recently made a state in the 20th century", added David. "Do you remember when Pontius Pilate wrote a placard for the cross of Jesus? asked David. It has been said that Pilate wrote "king of the Jews" on the placard, when in reality it read, "king of the Judaeans". Jesus never referred to himself as a Jew because he was not a Jew, he was a Judaean and referred to himself as such.

"Recess is nearly over, we have to get back to class", stated Joseph. "Okay", said David. "This has been a lot of good information; I will look further into it, by doing my own research", said Joseph.

"Yes, we will be discussing more of the evidence that proves what was presented is true; our identity has been hidden, but both our identity and history is being revealed," stated David.

"I'm excited to share more about our identity and history in the next class", exclaimed David. "We can't let Steven and Candace have all the fun; see you then!" laughed Joseph.

Tribe of

Judah

יהודה

About the Author

.

Dr. Vondell is a veteran of the U.S. Air Force where she worked as an Education Specialist. She has a Doctorate degree in Human Services, and a Master's and Bachelor's degree in Psychology with a Specialization in Marriage and Family Therapy. Dr. Vondell is an author, public speaker, and relationship consultant. She is travelling on the continent of Alkebulan/Afrika but resides in California, U.S.A.

Dr. Vondell is available for speaking engagements; she can be reached via WhatsApp at +233 20 880 9017 or at avondell7@gmail.com

www.ingramcontent.com/pod-product-compliance
Lightning Source LLC
LaVergne TN
LVHW080040170826
845677LV00025B/1927
9798374955743